ONE IN A MILLION

Dr. Charles L Pocock MBE

1924 -2002

First Published 2003

Homeleigh Books
Homeleigh
Marigold Lane
Stock
Ingatestone
Essex CM4 9PU

ISBN 0-9539082-1-6

Printed and Bound by
Doppler Press, Brentwood

FOREWORD

Sadly, Charles passed away on 16th December 2002 at the age of 78, soon after he completed the writing of this book, but before he had chosen a title. Consequently, "ONE IN A MILLION" is my choice, for a number of reasons.

Firstly, Charles's rare medical condition, Diastrophic Dysplasia, is estimated to occur only once in every million births.

In so many other ways he was truly **"ONE IN A MILLION".** No one could have had a more wonderful husband; he was always considerate, patient and kind, never selfish and never complaining, despite the many physical problems he had, especially in latter days.

I feel so proud and privileged to have been married to Charles, who is so greatly missed and who was such a fine example and inspiration to so many people.

I praise God for his life and pray that this little book "One in a Million" will be a blessing to family, friends and acquaintances alike.

Barbara M. Pocock

November 2003

CONTENTS

Introduction   1

Welsh Village Life   3

Life in Hospital   7

Towards Integration   10

 Into the World of Work   13

One in a Million   18

Spiritual Spur   22

Landmark   25

Mobility   28

International Year of the Disabled   34

Restricted Growth Association   43

Radio and Television   47

Up and Away   54

My Time at Remploy Ltd.   59

My Wonderful Family   63

INTRODUCTION

At various times during my life many people have suggested to me that I should write a book about my life, whilst others have offered the suggestion that I should "go into politics". The latter idea did not seem to me to hold out any prospect of permanent and gainful employment. Employment was a major socially concerning issue and this was certainly very much in my mind as a most important objective; in any case, I think I would have found it very stultifying to have to, stick to the "Party line"!. However, the "write your life story" idea has resulted in this little offering.

The words spoken to me when I became a Christian in 1947 are with me still: "The Lord is going to richly bless you in all that you do". At the time, in my severely disabled state, I thought it a rather strange thing to say to me.

The question may very well be asked, WHY write a book? Why indeed! Well, partly in justification for writing perhaps I should just mention at this very early stage in my narrative that my situation is and always has been anything but normal, or more accurately - average.

Therefore, as I enter the autumn years of my life, perhaps I owe it to posterity (family and friends really) to write down some of my thoughts and note some of the many exciting events that have amazingly littered my life with interest and challenge.

Standing at the beginning of the 21st century there is much talk and debate about social attitudes of the general public towards minority groups and people who might be described as disadvantaged; for example, black people, Asian people, poor people, illiterate people, disabled people .... the list could go on and on. Awareness of the needs of these groups and many others besides has grown apace in the last thirty years or so. However, we still have a long way to go. My little story (part social history) tells not only of the struggle (I don't much like that word) to make my way in life trying to cope with a world which, if not openly hostile, then certainly an unfriendly and puzzled society which caused me to move precariously and sometimes uncomfortably through the normal ups and downs of life without actually being able to conform to the accepted "average".

I dedicate this little book to my lovely, long-suffering wife and my patient and understanding daughters and their families.

Charles Pocock

WELSH VILLAGE LIFE

I was born on 29th October 1924 of extremely modest but proud parents; poverty was not uncommon in the mining valleys of South Wales in those seemingly far-off days. My father was an Englishman born in Lymington, Hampshire; perhaps he would be called a "Hampshire Hog"! His father (my grandfather) owned a little bakery which nestled in a lovely dell on the edge of the New Forest. My mother was Welsh and came from a little town called Pontardawe, near the somewhat larger City of Swansea.

My parents had met during the First Great War of 1914-1918. My mother was a cook, "in service" as it was called, in one of the big houses of the area. My father was in the Army and served in the 3rd Kings Own Huzzars. He fought in hand-to-hand combat in the infamous trenches of France and became a victim of the first gas bomb attack, as a result of which he was invalided out of the Army and eventually died in 1940 as a direct result of the gassing. After a prolonged legal battle my mother was ultimately awarded a very small War Widow's Pension.

My Mum and Dad had met during the War years when my father was on leave from the Army and decided to visit his sister, who was also "in service" in the same house where my mother was cook. They married in the 1920's and eventually set up their first (and only) home in the small and quiet mining village of Llandybie (the Church of St. Tybie) in the County of Carmarthenshire. They took something of a financial risk when they decided to buy a small semidetached three bedroom house, in the sense that there was no guarantee of secure long-term employment. The only way they could afford to buy the house was to borrow the money needed from the Local Authority - £400, which of course they had to pay back over an agreed period of time - this obviously gave greater importance to the need for employment. The price sounds unbelievably low in these days; nevertheless, it was a huge venture for my parents to embark upon on their low incomes and my father's indifferent health. The concept of working mothers was very much frowned upon in those days, and in any case my mother was fully occupied in looking after the home and bringing up the family of four children.

Llandybie was, and to some extent still is, a tightly-knit and quiet community of kind and warm-hearted people, and like many other Welsh villages it was characterised by the two Celtic features of coal mining and choral singing. The coal mine producing anthracite coal (known as the black diamond of Wales) dominated the village and its life. Choral singing (especially male voice), and chapel-going, played a very big part and greatly influenced the cultural life of the community. This would be true of many villages in South Wales at that time. Chapel-going was not so much an expected duty, but was accepted as an unquestioned part of Welsh village life. The coal mines have long since gone, but the chapel-going tradition falteringly lingers on. Inevitably, in such a culture and community, the men of the village were predominantly coal miners. There was very little else for men of working age to do other than working on the local farm, or doing casual work. The Llandybie colliery stood on the side of a hill on the fringe of the village, and the coal-dust "Tip" seemed to tower menacingly like a black mountain brooding over the little huddle of houses at the foot of this "mountain". Most of the miners lived in these houses; 1 can almost see them now, trudging their way home at the end of the working shift which was signalled by a loud hooter which could be heard across the village. For many of the wives the day was punctuated by the periodic howling of the hooter, saying "Put the kettle on" and "Get the bath water hot". Of course, there was no such thing as Pit Baths in those early days and the men would walk home in their coal-dust laden clothes, hands and faces blackened from long hours at the coal face. Washing bodies and clothes had to wait until the men arrived home to whatever washing facilities they had available. Very often it would be a tin bath placed on the hearth in front of a blazing coal fire in the living room; privacy and modesty were not high on the list of priorities!

I was very amused on one occasion when an Aunt and Uncle of mine paid us a visit from their home in Ealing, West London. My Dad had arranged to take Uncle Sid down the village mine to see the kind of conditions the men had to work in, as this would be a revelation to visitors from "The Smoke". The only thing that concerned my Dad, he not being a miner, was the fact that despite having spent a considerable length of time down the mine, he had emerged without a trace of coal-dust on his face, but my Uncle proudly displayed the evidence of his visit all over his face

As I mentioned, coal-mining and choral singing seemed to be the two lynch-pins that held this community together. As a youngster I was constantly urged to go to church and to Sunday School. My parents were loosely attached to the Church of England, and although they were certainly not regular attenders, we (as children) were encouraged to attend each week. The Church was set on a slight hill on the edge of the village and seemed to be keeping a concerned watch over the inhabitants.

When 1 was in my early twenties, and after becoming a committed Christian, I decided to join the little Salem Baptist Church in Campbell Road, Llandybie. I recall the building well. It was stone-built, one-roomed, with a small patch of lawn in the front. The building conceded nothing to creature comforts, and certainly technology had not reached any of the modern standards. Public address systems, overhead projectors and multi-media screens were but distant dreams, if they were thought about at all! In any case, Salem Church was too small for such equipment.

One mid-week meeting I attended was designated a "prayer meeting" during which various extemporary prayers were offered, interspersed by various members of the congregation standing up and reading or reciting passages of Scripture which had been "laid on their hearts" to share with the assembled gathering, usually no more than about 15 or 20 people. One dear elderly lady would often recite from memory a whole Psalm of a dozen or more verses - how sad to see that this practice has lapsed!

Interestingly enough, despite its mining character, Llandybie was judged to be one of the cleanest villages in the valleys of South Wales, at least as assessed by a local newspaper of the day. As previously mentioned, male voice singing played an almost indispensable part of the life of the population, and pleasingly strong echoes can still be heard to this day. It could almost be described as a kind of choral legacy for future generations One has only to think of a Welsh International Rugby match to be reminded of our rich heritage, as spontaneous choir singing breaks out (including four-part harmony) across the packed stands.

My brother, two sisters and I were brought up in this, not financially rich, but nevertheless secure, warm and stable environment. I believe that this stability and security provided by my parents played a major part in building our characters.

One of my dearest friends whilst I lived in South Wales, was, a young man named Keith Wyn Jones, whose father was the stationmaster at the Ammanford Railway Station. Keith and his father had seen me many times as I passed by driving my invalid carriage and each time Keith had got very excited. In the special "language" between father and son Keith would plead and pester his father leaving him in no doubt that he wanted an invalid carriage like mine. His father agreed, provided I would be prepared to teach Keith to drive. You see, Keith was a very severely disabled boy from birth. He was without speech or hearing, and his body was very badly malformed.

It was an amazing discovery I made when I found out that after the passing of each day the father would encourage the son to grunt and gesticulate his way through the days events. With great patience and love the father would then type the account of the day's doings, and carefully (almost laboriously) explain what the words meant and how the son should make an attempt to repeat the words that had been typed. Unintelligible to most, Keith would nevertheless try his very best to make noises approaching the sound of the words. Whenever we met on a dark winter's night Keith, always carried a small torch and would shine the light in my face so that he could 'see' what I was saying.

Through the encouragement of his father Keith became a Christian and would spend many days visiting clubs for the Hearing and Speech impaired people in order to share his faith with them.

I was much challenged and inspired by Keith and his saintly father who was a local preacher and hymn writer, and who left an enriching legacy to those who knew and loved him.

LIFE IN HOSPITAL

Of the four children born to my parents - two boys and two girls - two were perfectly fit (some would even say normal or average) and two were born with profound disabilities - that is, my sister Phyllis and I. We were, and indeed are, congenitally impaired, ie. present at birth, with a condition which was unrecognised then and therefore unnamed, but subsequently - with the advance of science and technology -was eventually identified and named as Diastrophic Dysplasia. I understand that the condition affects approximately one in every million births. This figure is not totally reliable since the condition is not a notifiable one, and this makes any attempt at accurate figures almost impossible. More about this a little later.

During my early years, childhood and adolescence, my rare and unusual disability meant that I spent broken periods of long-term hospitalisation. Due to the rarity of my disability and the seemingly huge lack of available medical knowledge about the affliction I was "stuck with", I was packed off to the one hospital where they thought they might be able to do something to correct or even modify my difficulties. This was the Sir Robert Jones and Agnes Hunt Orthopaedic Hospital in Oswestry, Shropshire. Similarly, my sister went through the same procedure.

From the quiet village where we were brought up, to the hospital in Oswestry, seemed a very long way to go in those days of slower traffic and no Motorways. By the time I was in hospital for my first long stay, my father had died, the effects of the War having finally caught up with him. Consequently, my mother was left to bring up the family of four children on extremely meagre financial means. The limitations of the financial purse meant that my poor mother could only afford to make one visit to the hospital to see me, and that visit obviously brought me much pleasure.

There were 25 patients on the ward of this rather large and somewhat barren hospital. which had an open air verandah all the way down one side. The routine was that after breakfast had been cleared away and all the medicines and treatments given, the beds were wheeled out on to the verandah, presumably so that we could benefit from the fresh air. To pass the time away we patients would devise all sorts of inventive games and activities. We would ask for a few of the beds to be pushed together so that we could somehow play shove ha'penny or some such game. The patients came from all parts of the country and we never knew who would be in the beds on either side, and certainly had no choice in the matter! I recall, during one of these game sessions, a ginger-haired lad somehow managed to make a catapult. He would scramble down to the bottom of the bed, from which position he threw breadcrumbs to the birds. How nice, you might think! However, he enticed the birds on to the verandah until they were within range, and would fire at them with his makeshift catapult. It makes me shudder as I recall this incident. What was his home background like and what were the other influences on his young life which may have been responsible for producing such an aggressive and unhealthy streak in him?. What did the future hold for him, I wondered.

After undergoing a fairly major hip operation, the nurses - so I was told afterwards -had some difficulty in "bringing me round". I emerged from the fog induced by the anaesthetic only to discover that my whole body, apart from my head and arms, was encased in a heavy plaster-cast. I soon discovered that I could do very little for myself bound tightly in this plaster jacket. I remember the Ward Sister trying to bring me out of the anaesthetic with teaspoons of brandy, which one would have thought would have the opposite effect. However, the treatment seemed to do the trick and I discovered that not only was I in this confined plaster cast but that the cast was soaked with my own blood from the surgery.

When, after 14 months, I was discharged from hospital, my mother made the journey from Llandybie to Oswestry to take me home. Having spent a fairly long time on a long, airy ward, shouting to my fellow-patients, I wasn't aware of how loud I was talking. My brother and sisters were eagerly awaiting my return home and there was a great deal of excited chatter on my arrival. My mother kept telling me to keep my voice down and not to shout. It took some time for me to adjust to the confines of the small rooms in our house after being in a large hospital ward. On coming home again, it was a relief to have some ease from the discomfort I had been suffering, including the occasional locking of my hip joint which used to occur at inopportune times.

As I leave behind these few glimpses of my intermittent hospital stays, I reflect that they took place at a time in my life when I would normally be receiving formal education, which by these visits was severely interrupted and impaired. Certainly in those earlier years of my life, i.e. the 1920's and 1930's there were very poor and limited opportunities to pursue any meaningful academic studies and education, especially for anyone confined to a hospital bed for many months. Indeed, I was in that position, spending long months in hospital every year or so. My "education" in hospital consisted of knitting tea-cosies and making raffia teapot stands rather than being taught any of the normal academic subjects such as Mathematics, English, Geography and the like.

In later years, as you will read, I went on to do a great deal of public speaking on topics relating to disability and integration, and I would sometimes refer to those hospital stays and claim, correctly, that I had no academic qualifications, but I did have a drawer full of tea-cosies! I sometimes describe myself as a self-made man, in response to which some might mutter "he could have made a better job of it". Well, maybe so, maybe.

TOWARDS INTEGRATION

From these relatively unpromising beginnings it can readily be appreciated that my education could not be described as formal or indeed normal; in fact it was limited in the extreme. As I grew into adulthood I became increasingly aware of the fact that this lack of a good educational base, not surprisingly, had a most profound impact on my hopes for future employment. I very quickly realised that my job prospects were indeed grim and the outlook bleak. Added to this backdrop was the fact that few people of moderate social standing believed that I would be capable of making any meaningful contribution. Judgement of my potential abilities were likely to be on what I looked like rather than what I might be able to do. Vestiges of that tendency tenaciously linger on!! Assessed on that negative criteria it seemed to me that I stood no chance at all. I was and still am very short and quite badly deformed - would I become an embarrassment to any employer who took the "risk" of engaging me in whatever capacity? I was, over and over again, given the distinct impression that I had little or no potential of any worth. I was strongly encouraged to accept my lot and "not to worry". You don't have to concern yourself about earning a living; we'll look after you and care for you", they said. 1 almost gave in and believed them, but this was not the strong advice my father gave me. Of course, he was anxious about my future, but he said to me more than once: "Charles, if you don't help yourself, no-one is going to do it for you". "Be independent, boy", he would passionately urge me - a piece of fatherly advice that has had a profound impact on all that I have tried to do in my life, and his words still colour what I say and do.

The Bible says something similar: 'The things that are impossible with men are possible with God". That tells me that there are some things that are possible with men. I should do what 1 can and should encourage those who are facing similar difficulties to do the same.

Current trends and the voices of disabled people at the beginning of the 21st Century show me how very much ahead of his day my father was in terms of his attitude to me and my disability. My father died in the mid 1940's but he left behind an abiding legacy and a challenge to live by. In those far off days disability was not something one readily acknowledged or recognised. It was not a subject that was talked about other than behind closed doors and in whispered voices. There was little or no disability awareness or Lobby at that time. The voice of disabled people was silent, particularly in those places where opinion-forming and social policy planning was taking place. I wanted to explore whether I might be able to play a part in changing the policy and planning from a dependency culture to independence. Social policy seemed to reinforce the culture of dependency. There was little or no provision for further education, skill training, or even craft training. Independence for disabled people seemed not to be a legitimate objective to be aspired to - a "no go" area indeed! Disabled people were not only being lulled into a state of passivity, but their own individual expectations were being depressed to the point where they could almost be described as "passengers of life". Carried along to an unknown destination by those who thought they knew what was good and "best for them", and who seemed to say they knew where disabled people ought to be, neither seen or heard. After all, it was far less embarrassing and more conveniently comfortable (for society) if disabled people were persuaded to accept and believe that they had neither a role, or rights in the life of their community, of which they were uncomfortably a part. Their place was to remain silent and grateful.

Challenging this attitude was the pioneer and campaigner, Lord Morris of Wythenshaw who, prior to his elevation to the House of Lords, was affectionately known as Alf. Morris, MP., in the late 1960's and 70's. Alf and his colleague, a writer named Arthur Butler, wrote a book about the problems of disability and the need to pass an Act of Parliament called "The Chronically Sick and Disabled Persons Act, 1970". The book is entitled "No Feet to Drag" and is described by Duncan Guthrie (the then Director of the National Fund for Research into Crippling Diseases) as "a fascinating study of the problems of disablement in this country". The book provides case histories and thumbnail sketches of significant personalities both from the Parliamentary field and the growing voluntary sector in British life. Duncan Guthrie says "the steady pressure and dedication that is being applied to get a better deal for disabled people means that the picture is constantly changing".

I sometimes shared the public platform with Lord Alf. Morris. He was asked on one occasion why he called his book "No Feet to Drag. He explained that he had been very disappointed by the very slow passage of the Bill through Parliament - members of Parliament had been dragging their feet.

One of Alf Morris's constituents, who was a double lower limb amputee, said in response to this explanation for the title of the book - "They're very lucky to have any feet to drag".

In his research for the book, Arthur Butler twice visited my home in Wickford, Essex and spent some hours talking through my own experiences and we also considered together what impact those experiences had had on my attitude to my life and how they had significantly influenced my personal philosophy of life, and also gave some expression to the hopes about the role and place in society which should be occupied by our disabled colleagues, who are after all (or should be) part of our community.

The message that things and policies had to change was well-supported by some strong and influential Parliamentary colleagues and friends from the voluntary sector. By the end of 1970 we had reached an important stage in our campaigning, as up to that point we had never met or had any meaningful discussions with any Government departments. We had been obliged to deal only with what they called "Junior Ministers". However, on 7th December 1970 I led a small deputation to a meeting at No. 10 Downing Street - the first of several visits. I was not alone but was accompanied by a small group of colleagues and friends such as Alf Morris MP., James Loring (the then Director of the Spastics Society - now called Scope) and four cross-Party members of Parliament. The Prime Minister at the time was Rt. Hon. Edward Heath, who gave the deputation a fair hearing and seemed to have a good grasp of the issues we were promoting. He certainly did not brush us aside or lightly dismiss us.

Not all disabled people agreed with or supported this call for greater independence. I believe that there is a sense in which the issues of disability have parallels with the "race issues". What we were seeking to achieve was not preferential treatment but rather equality of opportunity, similar to that enjoyed by most other people. These were precisely the sentiments and objectives set out (eventually) in The Chronically Sick and Disabled Persons Act of 1970.

It took a long time for the spirit of the disabled population to be roused from the state of enforced passivity and begin to vocalise their long suppressed aspirations. My father's maxim of some years earlier came back to me again and again, "if you don't do it for yourself then it won't be done". It seemed to me that ignorance and prejudice had clouded society's vision and consequently limited their expectations as to what might be achieved by disabled people if only they were given the appropriate training and right opportunities.

INTO THE WORLD OF WORK?

All the pressure around suggested that at a certain age people should start thinking about earning a living and "paying one's way". I saw other youngsters growing up and getting a job and eventually getting married and settling down. My prospects did not look too promising! In fact, 1 got the distinct impression that no one in my village had any real expectations for me so far as working for wages was concerned. This seemed to be the attitude of society generally, disabled people might be seen but not heard, and definitely not employed. This unspoken attitude conveyed itself powerfully to me, but nevertheless I pressed on. It seemed that the odds were stacked against me but I felt I had to resist the notion that if you are disabled then your lot in life is to be a "passenger" rather than a participator. I had seen my father languish "on the dole" before he died. Getting some kind of work was becoming more and more an urgent necessity, not only for my own self-respect but more importantly to try and give my widowed mother some financial help with the housekeeping costs. I was getting to the stage where I would accept any sort of job.

Obviously it had to be a sitting-down job, and office work seemed to be the most suitable, so I enrolled as a student at a very small, one-man school, rather grandly called Pagefield College in the town of Ammanford, about three miles from my home. By this time I had acquired a hand-propelled invalid carriage, paid for by the generosity of the village folk. It was ironically called by its manufacturers in Bath a "Ride-in-ease"! It was anything but easy to hand-pedal this masterpiece of engineering the three miles to college. The road was hilly and my arms were short, but I pressed on. Exposed to all weather I would often arrive at College having been soaked en route and as I sat in class my clothes would be giving off little puffs of steam as I dried out! There were only about a dozen students taught by its one and only teacher and College owner, a man of very strange and quaint mannerisms with an odd sense of humour. The subjects covered were Book-keeping, Shorthand

and Typewriting, with some very basic Mathematics thrown in. My resulting typewriting skill I felt I could put to some profitable use, but who would take me on? Somehow the news got around that I could type and I was approached by someone in the village asking whether I could type up a manuscript of a book about the Aztec Indians. My typewriter at the time was not the most modern, but I rattled away on the old machine for about three weeks. When I completed the work and handed it in, he offered profuse thanks and the princely sum of £2.50, which was even a pittance in those long ago days. However, it seemed like manna from heaven to me - well, maybe not from heaven! I handed it over to my mother with a real sense of pride, as this was the first time I had been able to help with the housekeeping. It was quite an exciting moment which seemed to hold out a flickering prospect of better things ahead.

I then got a job (a sort of "out of the kindness of the heart" job) working for a local Doctor. I think he had heard about me from his neighbour who wrote the book about the Aztec Indians. By the time I got this little job I had become motorised via an invalid tricycle, purchased for me by the Local Authority. It was powered by a 125ce engine and rather ironically called a Barrett Midget, and was made by a firm in Bristol. It had a fibreglass body and ran on a mixture of petrol and oil. I often wonder why equipment for the disabled does not appear to be made to the highest specification as other goods are? The engine of this little machine was mounted at the rear of the centrally positioned seat (it was only a single seater). Rider and engine were exposed to the vagaries of the weather, which often affected the efficiency of both. The Barrett often proved very difficult to get started and I would therefore keep it going when I parked outside the Doctor's Surgery when I started work for the day, as I was never sure that I would be able to get it started again. The Doctor was not the least bit impressed with my explanation and with obvious irritation in his voice he said sternly: "You look as if you are ready to go home before you've even started work, young man". He was looking out through the Surgery window at my transport noisily pop-popping away and belching out clouds of bluish-grey exhaust fumes while I was working. This short-lived job came to a not unexpected end within a few months.

These work skirmishes were interspersed by bouts of unemployment until in January 1948 I obtained a full-time position as shorthand-typist to the County Surveyor in the town of Carmarthen. This gentleman was an old-fashioned strict disciplinarian, held in awe by his staff, including me. Late one mid-winter afternoon when the light was fading in the office, the

Boss barked out: "Pocock, put the light on as you leave". I trembled as I looked up at the switch which was definitely out of my reach. There was no way I could do what he asked me , but how could I tell this severe gentleman that I couldn't reach? However, I had to, and was then scared of his reaction, but what a pleasant surprise! This harsh-mannered man seemed to melt under his own embarrassment. "Oh, I'm so sorry", he said. He got to his feet and towering over me put the light on himself and even held the door open to see me out. I learned a valuable lesson that day. How can we who are disabled expect others to know of our difficulties if we never get the opportunity to tell them and show them. I hope my boss learned a little from that incident too. I am absolutely sure that there is a fund of goodwill out there in the community just waiting to be tapped in the kindest and gentlest way. After about three or four months in that job, and as I grew in confidence and ability, I felt it was time to move on and face new challenges.

I then secured a position as an Administrative Assistant at the old Ministry of National Insurance in the nearby town of Ammanford, and held this position for five years. I was learning all the time and absorbing these disciplines like a piece of blotting paper - not only administrative skills but social and communication skills too.

I was beginning to see, experience and live like the average (normal) person. Then, like bolt out of the blue, my whole world seemed to collapse around me as I was called into the Head's office and handed my notice. The job that seemed so secure had finished. Mentally I floundered, and like a sinking man I thrashed around in my mind wondering what 1 was going to do.

Undaunted, but a little shaken by this experience, I applied immediately for an advertised post of General Clerk at an Agricultural College. The College, named in Welsh "Gelli Aur", meaning Golden Grove, was set in 420 acres of beautiful countryside. The building was in fact the old country seat of Lord Cawdor, and one felt quite grand working in such beautiful surroundings with its manicured lawns and vast array of flowering bushes and shrubs. There were three staff members serving the needs of the academic lecturing staff and 40 residential students. I spent ten relatively happy years at this College and of course I was learning all the time. I had an unexpressed sense that I was being prepared for some future work, yet unknown to me, and towards the end of the ten-year period I had a growing unsettled feeling. I felt I had to go, but where?

Disabled people were beginning to express their dissatisfaction with the way things were and started to explore ways of trying to change the minds of those who had some authority and could possibly do something about changing the way things were. However, they would need to be willing to change their own rather stereotyped attitude towards the nuisance factor of disabled people. I too was stirred and my Christian faith seemed to suggest to me that I too had some kind of responsibility to try and facilitate a fairly major shift in society's attitude towards those who, for whatever reason, appeared different from the average. There seemed a great tendency to judge things and people on the basis of what they looked like and this to me did not conform to what the Bible said - No-one is insignificant or unimportant. There is real value in everyone.

So I was stirred, and to some extent excited, by the thought that I could, maybe, have a part to play in bringing about an attitudinal change. Just maybe! I didn't know how but I was challenged by the possibility of influencing people's way of thinking.

We would have to become a front-line force if we were going to have any impact on the thinking of people and the need for fundamental change in that thinking process. How could we be involved in this "movement for change"? I didn't know. Born and brought up in the Welsh valleys, it all seemed a different world from where the seat of power and policy making was taking place.

At my desk, in the early days of my efforts to forge a career in the Golden Grove Agricultural College where I was a mere clerk/typist, for approximately ten years.

Jack Blake

A device I designed for my office use. It was named "Portasteps" because it was to fold down and be carried like a portmanteau. It was quite cold up there!

ONE IN A MILLION

Perhaps I should digress for a moment or two whilst I explain the occasional references to my disability. I make these references, certainly not to encourage the reader to feel "sympathy" for me, but rather to place on record something of my condition and situation, because I am very aware of the fact that there is not much information available about my condition, nor indeed about the total life impact it has had on me and my lifestyle.

1 know the title "One in a Million" sounds rather pompous, and for this I apologise! However, my condition - eventually identified as Diastrophic Dysplasia - means that a child is born with the condition at the rate of one in about every million live births. I call it my Double "D", as the full description is a bit of a mouthful.

When I was born in the mid-20's, there was considerable uncertainty and not a little confusion about the diagnosis. Often, in those early days, I was described as suffering from Achondroplasia, but I subsequently learned that my condition was even more rare. The "one in a million" tag means that there are only about 100 people in the population of Great Britain suffering from Diastrophic Dysplasia, and it is for this reason that I write in some detail about my situation and experiences. Boring possibly, but I feel it to be fairly important for the future. There was very little knowledge or clinical experience that the medical profession could call on to assist in the diagnosis in my case, and entering the 21st Century there is still a shortage of reliable statistical evidence, which in itself compounds the difficulty. Assuming that there are 30,000 General Practitioners in the country, it will readily be appreciated that only one GP. in 10 will ever encounter one person with the Double "D" condition in the whole of their Practice life.

The progress that has been made in medical knowledge and diagnostic techniques is to be welcomed, but from my perspective I would have to say that it has been painfully slow (literally). I want to continue to play my part in nudging things forward, mindful of the need to provide for and protect those who will certainly come after me. It is extremely exciting that new, bright and academically well qualified people have entered the arena of research and investigation.

Well now, what about the actual effect of my unique condition? What does it feel like and how has it developed through the years? What kind of impact has it had on my lifestyle? By now I have had well over 70 years experience and I can say that the condition has left me with a legacy of many complex problems of varying kinds and resultant malformations. The condition was present at birth (congenital) and I would say that the most obvious and curiosity-evoking element is the fact that I did not grow very tall! In fact, I am four feet and one inch tall (or short), whichever way you see me. I think that to describe myself as just over four feet tall, is not only statistically accurate, but is also a more positive description, whilst at the same time not denying the reality. What did Robert Burns say? "If we could see ourselves as others see us" I have always been left in no doubt about how others see me; however, I have always tried to see myself as God sees me, and others, as precious and loved, and that has always given me courage.

The condition has affected most, if not all, of the bony structure of my body, but the resulting malformation has been somewhat irrational. What has happened to one side of my body has not necessarily occurred on the other, and not to the same extent . The medical man may tell me why it is like that, all I know is that it is so. Two individuals with the same condition - for example, my sister Phyllis and I - do not necessarily display all the same characteristics. There are, however, some similar features. I am slightly taller than my sister, but whereas she has a straight spine mine has quite a severe curvature. The effect on my left hand is not the same as that on my right. Some of my joints are locked solidly but some are not. Most joints work very poorly and some not at all. Even those joints that once worked, albeit poorly, earlier in my life, have gradually got worse and eventually given up altogether. I record this by way of fact only, and certainly not to evoke sympathy or to portray myself as some "courageous cripple", which I definitely am not. The joint problems are often accompanied by unrelieved pain in various degrees. Sympathy and courageous tags are not sentiments that are compatible with my striving after independence.

One thing is certain - there has been no way out of my predicament. There is no balm or medical intervention that is ever likely to rectify the situation or substantially change the predicted prognosis. I have had to learn to live with it and in it, and at the same time endeavour to rise above the difficulties it has created, using the only resources available to me - my mind, spirit and, of course, my tongue!

But all is not lost, it very rarely is - and my life has been full of challenge and excitement; it has been positively rewarding for me, and hopefully for some of the many individuals from all parts of the world and from all walks of life who have crossed my path down through the years. But more of that a little later.

I understand from some of my medical friends, and I do have a few, that my condition presented itself as a result of what some call "spontaneous mutation", that is where both parents (unknown to themselves) were carriers of the guilty gene and then went on to produce a child. In that situation, the chances of the resulting birth presenting with the "Double D" condition are extremely high indeed. However, when only one parent (it matters not which) carries the guilty gene, then there is no greater chance of the couple producing an affected child than any other set of parents. The great mystery is that no-one will ever know who carries the responsible gene, or not unless there were to be a mass screening process. With such a very rarely occurring condition, the likelihood of such a screening programme being set up would be cost-prohibitive, but that would be the only way to protect against the possibility of the condition ever happening.

Social Impact

So, what effect has it had on my social life? Well, I certainly cannot be described as tall, dark and handsome! Perhaps two out of three is not bad - so take your pick! I can't even guess what I would have been had I not been the one in a million. In any event I ended up (or down, whichever way you care to view me) at the dizzy height of four feet one inch - I insist on the one inch, for obvious reasons. I wouldn't be without it.

The social impact of being so short and malformed tends to attract unwelcome and overt attention. People react in different ways when confronted by the unusual. Just as one small example - I remember driving my car in North London and stopping outside a newsagents, when I noticed a car had pulled up behind mine. The card contained four or five teenagers, dressed in "trendy gear". When they saw me they began to snigger and pointed fingers of scorn in my direction. They were taken by surprise as I strolled (perhaps staggered would be a better description of my gait) over to their car. They wound down the window, and I leaned into the car and suggested to them that they should consider the possibility of one day producing a child with my condition. I suggested to them that they might have a different attitude towards their own disabled child. Their faces dropped as I wished them good-day, went back to my car and drove off.

My parents knew nothing about the cause of my condition. It certainly took them both by surprise and created huge psychological, medical and financial problems, which had life-long ramifications. The rarity of the condition has created its own difficulties. After all, it is neither popular nor cost-effective to devote scarce resources to the pursuit of medical research into an infrequently occurring condition., but I hope that someone, someday will - although I recognise the rather discouraging economic arguments. I thought at least that it may be interesting, if not helpful, to share with the reader something of what it is like from the inside, as it were. Here I record some answers, factually and without sentimentality.

As I cast my mind back over the years and remember the village of my birth, my childhood is full of happy memories. There was a total lack of any negative references to the fact that my sister and I were different. The villagers knew our little family well and accepted us as full members of the community. My life experience tells me that it is society which relentlessly reminds us and me in particular of my physical limitations - as though I need any reminding. Sure, there are limitations, but don't we all have these at various times and in differing degrees. I mean, that's life after all. But it is what you do with what you've got that really matters.

SPIRITUAL SPUR

It was rather strange that during the last two years or so of my time at Golden Grove, the pleasant conditions at the College could not dim the growing frustration and dissatisfaction. I was beginning to realise that there were, so I felt, many more things that I could be doing with my life other than merely typing letters and filing correspondence. Possibly there were things that I could do beyond the typewriter keyboard - things that would be more meaningful, worthwhile and personally rewarding. On reflection, a review of my life up to that particular point would show just how cramped and limited it really was. If I had asked myself the question, "What do you expect from life?" I would have had to reply - "Nothing"; and that was a most unsatisfactory response. The conclusion of that little life review left me longing to break out of the cocoon of ignorance and prejudice with its limitations, and destroy the chains that seemed to be holding me back from responding to the opportunities that I felt were urging me forward.

The beautifully cultivated and neatly trimmed lawns, shrubs and flower beds, with meandering pathways through the lovely grounds of Golden Grove College were like a piece of heaven, and in so many ways I was sad to leave the place, but I was in danger of taking root there. However, I had to move on.

By this time I had decided to join the little Baptist Church in Llandybie, and then attended quite regularly. As I have mentioned, Chapel-going was a pretty important part of Sunday life. Eventually, I made a personal decision to respond to the Gospel and become a committed Christian. This happened after attending an Evangelical Mission held in the Bethany Methodist Church in nearby Ammanford. The Mission was run by young students who were all members of the Inter Varsity Fellowship. The invitation to attend the Mission came about one afternoon whilst I was sitting in my invalid carriage watching a local cricket match. As I sat there it started to rain (as it often seems to in Wales) . Suddenly a young man approached me, put his raincoat over my shoulders, and told me about the Mission and about his Christian faith. I immediately warmed to this young man and accepted his invitation to attend one of the meetings. Incidentally, prior to this, although I was an Anglican as were my parents, I had no sense of any personal commitment to Christ - in fact, I had never been inside a Nonconformist church in my life. I said I would attend the Mission, and I did. This was the spiritual spur that was to change my perspective on life, and the value of each human being . That is not to say that I was there and then made perfect - far from it - but my feet were set firmly on the way, Chapel-going took on a whole new meaning for me and I started attending regularly and was eager to learn more about my new-found faith. I was an avid learner as I travelled around the area looking for "good preachers and Bible teachers". The hymns we sang also took on a whole new meaning and seemed to speak to me directly. I loved the company of like-minded people and, in truth, "all things became new". I soon joined the Church Youth Group and would often go with them when they visited other Church groups. It was on one of these visits that I met, courted and eventually married my wife, Barbara, in 1957. We've been together for over 40 years now "and it don't seem a day too much". Much to the surprise of some early day sceptics, we have survived despite the normal ups and downs encountered by most other families; we have a strong mutual Christian faith that binds us together in love. We were sure that we had been brought together by the Lord and we trusted Him fully to care for us and protect us. Has it all been a bed of roses? No,. certainly not. Our faith has not shielded us from the hard knocks that life brings to most of us, but our faith has been our strength in all circumstances.

What my faith has not done, notwithstanding what some so-called Christians claim, it has not made me whole and released from the shackles of my disability. It has, however, given me the faith to see the real me, as God sees me. The Bible gives us this promise: "When we see Him we shall be like Him".

When Barbara and I got married we bought a small semi-detached house in the town of Ammanford. As the years slipped quietly and pleasantly by we were blessed with two little girls, separated by a couple of years. Can you possibly imagine our joy (mine in particular) when the girls were born without a blemish and with no hint of my sort of condition.

How blessed we were and are! I remember almost bursting with pleasure and pride when the girls were babies and I took them for a walk in the pram.

I could hardly see where I was going as I looked over the handle of the pram, but that didn't matter, my joy was un-contained! Our little family of four was now complete and I vowed to give my wife and girls all the love and security that I had enjoyed so lavishly bestowed by my parents.

Can you share with me the joy and thrill as I began to see life in a new way, with new values? I no longer saw my disability but only the person whom God loves. My conversion heightened my concern for people and the quality and condition of their lives, particularly those who were having to cope with some physical problem or another. I felt that I was able to empathise with them out of my own experience, both of faith and disability, and I began to try and bring help and hope in a world that is pretty confusing.

(L) My strong support. My wife Barbara and I outside my brothers home just before our marriage in August 1957 (Ready for what life may have in store for us)

(R) A picnic pause. A little snap of my sister Phyllis and I as we pause for this hillside picnic, taken soon after the birth of our first daughter, Helen. She sleeps safely in the sunshine. This is a medically interesting photograph, bearing in mind that my medical condition occurs only once in every million live births. My sister now lives in a Cheshire home in South Wales, and now depends on a wheelchair.

LANDMARK

I looked around and realised that my contemporaries had moved on in their lives. I, however, seemed to have reached the full extent of my stifled "career", and then in 1963 my whole life suddenly took an entirely new course, which to me was totally unexpected. The year of 1963 was indeed to become a landmark year in my life. Sharing in what was to become, for me certainly, a momentous time were my dear wife and two very young children; challenging, and indeed a life-changing experience.

This was not only an exciting time but also I decided to move from the familiar and secure Welsh village life to Wickford in Essex, which is within fairly comfortable driving distance of London. It was a move I felt compelled to make, and London was , of course, the place where things seemed to he happening! The reason for this major move was because I had managed to obtain a position as Chief Executive of a National Charity dealing with the mobility needs of disabled people and trying to help solve their problems. I had a real feeling of eager anticipation as I viewed the prospect of being able to break out of the limiting straight-jacket I had been tied into thus far. I felt I had been suffocated by the overbearing constraints of people's goodness to me, and the job prospect in London seemed to lure me forward; it was an opportunity I felt I should not let slip by. Of course, leaving the safety and security of life in Wales was a challenge to us as a family; it would be worth saying here that without the support and unquestioning loyalty of Barbara I could not have pursued my dream.

With my new found faith the move to London was not only exciting but a real test of that faith. Whilst I firmly believe that God is the God of the impossible, I also believe that we have to do the possible. I sometimes feel that we tend to shirk our own responsibility and expect others or God to intervene to make up for our own slothfulness. But I'm beginning to sound too sanctimonious!

I had heard that there was soon to be advertised the position of General Secretary of the Disabled Drivers' Association, which had offices in East London. I was already Group Secretary of the Ammanford local branch so was quite knowledgeable about the main policy of the Organisation. Having bought a small car from the sale of my home in Llandybie (my mother having died in January 1956) we travelled to London, which was quite an adventure in those days. My first visit to London was for my interview, which took place at the Greenwich Seaman's Hospital situated near the famous Cutty Sark on the Thames Embankment. I remember the day well; it was one of those rather rare beautiful days with blue sky and warm sunshine. Barbara and the girls decided that, whilst I was attending the interview, they would explore the Cutty Sark and do some shopping. We agreed to meet up later in the day when we judged the interviews would be over. This experience of travelling to London, attending the interview in front of a panel of eight people, and in the rather imposing and historic Seaman's Hospital, was all rather overwhelming - but I pressed on. I really can't remember how many candidates had been short-listed for the position but I was told that there had been 55 completed application forms. What became patently obvious was the fact that I was the only disabled candidate. I didn't know whether this was a good thing or not. In any event I was determined not to use my disability to gain any unfair advantage over the other candidates - after all, wasn't I committed to true integration? I believed then, and still do today, that "ability to do the job" should be the main criteria as to suitability.

I heaved a huge sigh of relief when the interview was over. In closing the interview the Chairman of the panel, himself a severely disabled gentleman, turned to me and said that he would not allow the panel's decision to be in any way influenced one way or the other by the fact of my disability. That was exactly how I wanted to be treated by no favours or any preferential treatment, but just judged on merit alone like everybody else. For better or worse! Anyway, a few days later I received a letter from the panel Chairman complimenting me on my interview performance, but regrettably having to inform me that I had come a very close second! I was naturally disappointed and a little deflated because I had held high expectations that this job was for me, but I thought "Oh well, so be it". Imagine my delight and surprise when in a couple of days a second letter came from the Chairman to say that the person who had beaten me to the post had changed his mind and was unable to accept. The job was therefore being offered to me! Was this some sort of divine intervention, I wondered? With such unexpected twists the course of our lives can be dramatically changed.

With a good deal of excitement I accepted the job, and as a family we prepared to leave South Wales and set out on this new challenging chapter of our lives. It was a real test of our family love and devotion, as we certainly had no idea what the future had in store for us.

My old and very good friend Gwyn Matthias (now deceased) when I lived in Ammanford, Carmarthenshire. We stand proudly alongside our invalid carriages as we prepare to set off on our first ever long journey. Well it was very long when compared to our driving experience. We were setting out to attend our first Annual General Meeting of the then Invalid Tricycle Association, at the Alexandra Palace in North London. In fact we were so apprehensive about driving into London in our invalid carriages that we enlisted the assistance of the Automobile Association to pilot us in to my Aunt's flat in Ealing West London where we were due to spend the three nights of the A.G.M. at the Ally Pally - as we called it.

MOBILITY

The offices of the Disabled Drivers' Association were housed in a rather poor prefabricated building in the East End of London. My strong Welsh accent seemed to clash with the equally strong Cockney accent of the area.

However, I found that the true Eastenders were very kind and friendly and were anxious to do whatever they could to help me settle in to the new job. I think some of them must have realised that 1 was somewhat at sea in these unfamiliar surroundings. I set about the task of getting to grips with the work, getting to know the staff, and helping them get to know this total stranger they had inherited - a bit of a challenge for them too!

As I say, the offices were housed in a rather run-down prefabricated building that had seen better days. It sat on a small patch of what appeared to be "no man's land" behind a red-bricked industrial building. Architecturally impressive it was not; nonetheless, it was the Head Office of this emerging National Organisation which sought to serve the mobility needs of disabled people across the nation. The Disabled Drivers' Association had, prior to 1963, been called the Invalid Tricycle Association, and changing the name was one of the first big tasks I was required to do. With a subscribing membership of some 8,000 and with 75 local groups scattered across the country the task necessitated a great deal of travelling in my little mini-car. I started a three-year programme of visiting all 75 local groups in order to encourage a more cohesive body with stronger communication links throughout the Association. As I toured the country, meetings were arranged for me to address gatherings both of disabled people and also Local Authority representatives and people from other organisations. This gave me the opportunity to promote and reinforce the Organisation's policy, the main thrust of which was to encourage independence through personal mobility; this personal mobility was the key to the door of independence and integration. The pursuit of this main objective meant that for the first time in my life I found myself in situations that required speaking for and on behalf of disabled people who felt they had no voice, as we endeavoured to lobby and negotiate with Ministers of various Government departments.

One of the worthwhile aspects of the job was dealing with the flood of daily correspondence from people from all walks of life, and in various ways needing someone with whom to share their difficulties. The problems with which I was confronted ranged widely from, for example, the dear elderly lady who wanted some help in dealing with her Local Authority concerning planning permission for the building of a small garage in which to house her Government-issued invalid tricycle, to the case of a young man who lived in a small rented flat where he was regularly disturbed by the people in the flat overhead, whose bumping, banging and loud music destroyed his peace. In both these cases, and very many others, the problems were quickly resolved after I sent appropriately worded letters on their behalf. Although these issues had no direct relevance to mobility they did have an adverse effect on the lives of the two persons concerned. These matters and others like them only served to demonstrate how complex and involved is the consequence of disability.

The problems of access to public buildings, parking problems and such like complaints landed like a snowfall of confetti on my desk week after week. As this work developed my knowledge also increased, as did my confidence in dealing with them. The various concerns affecting the lives of people with disabilities became more and more focused on my heart. My experience of disability gave me a great deal of understanding as I tried to sit where they sat, see as they did and feel as they themselves felt. I felt a great empathy with my fellows.

Public speaking became quite an important feature of the work I was trying to do and as a Welshman I very much enjoyed this aspect of my work. Although, as I mentioned earlier, I had very meagre education and certainly no training in public speaking, I nevertheless revelled in these opportunities. I enjoyed and still do enjoy the art of marshalling the English language in such a way that influences and persuades. I was sometimes described by some who heard me as the David Lloyd George of the Association! That was quite a compliment but I'm not sure that it was an accurate description; I certainly didn't have Lloyd George's hair that seemed to go with his eloquence!

Mobility and the freedom to become personally mobile, by whatever means, became a dominant feature of the campaigning. Every possible and legitimate means was used to publicise and promote the work of my

Organisation. In pursuit of this policy I had to organise what was called the Trafalgar Square Rally, staged in an area which had been closed off to the general public, around Nelson's Column. Barriers were erected to keep the general public out and protect the assembled disabled people on the inside.

Tremendous support was given by a host of individuals and organisations such as the Metropolitan Police, Red Cross and St. John's Ambulance. There was an impressive array of speakers gathered on the platform including such people as Alf. Morris MP., James Loring, the then Director of Scope, and Neil Marten MP. (who played a key role in assisting the setting-up of the All-Party Disablement Group in the House of Commons). Following the speeches I was proud to be able to lead a deputation to No. 10 Downing Street to meet the then Prime Minister (The Rt. Hon. Mr. Edward Heath, MP.), and I some months later headed a delegation to No. 10. We met in the august atmosphere of the Cabinet Room at No. 10 and I sat directly opposite Mr. Heath, flanked on either side by two Officer colleagues from the DDA. The Prime Minister had a clear grasp of the issues we were raising with him, and we felt we had been given a very fair and attentive hearing.

This was only one of a variety of events that we staged as there became a growing public awareness of our "Cause", and hopefully we could persuade the Government into some kind of helpful response.

Jack Blake

I always looked up to my friend (the late) Graham Hill. He and I, and an unnamed London Policeman met at Horse Guards Parade just prior to a meeting I had arranged with the then Prime Minister, The Rt. Hon. Edward Heath MP at No. 10 Downing Street. I was to lead a deputation to the Prime Minister on behalf of the Disabled Drivers Association to press the case for better mobility provisions for very severely disabled people in the UK.

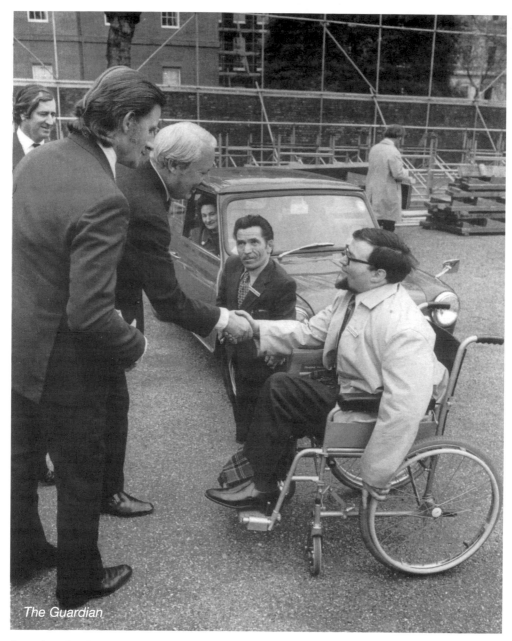

Greeting the Prime Minister in Horseguards Parade with Graham Hill in attendance. Campaigner - Peter MacBride (in the wheelchair) and myself standing by ready to continue our discussion in No.10.

Sport & General

Mr N. G. Carmichael MP, Parliamentary Secretary to the Minister of Transport (in 1968) accepted an invitation from the Disabled Driver's Association, to test drive an invalid tricycle, at Blue Star House Highgate Hill, London N19. Mr Carmichael seen talking to Charles (General Secretary of the Disabled Drivers' Association)

INTERNATIONAL YEAR OF THE DISABLED

I had the pleasure, indeed privilege, of getting to know a good cross-section of members of Parliament in the House of Commons, and lesser number in the House of Lords. In my representation work I spent quite a lot of my time attending the Houses of Parliament; in fact, the Gatekeepers in those days would recognise my car and flag me straight through the Courtyard to the special parking area. If I was to name one who for me ranked among the best and most loyal supporters, it would be Lord Alfred Morris of Wythenshaw. He was the world's first Minister for Disabled People. In 1981, whilst he was still a Member of Parliament and served as a constituency M.P., he persuaded the United Nations to declare the year of 1981 as The International Year of Disabled People. This was no mean achievement. Alf, as he was affectionately known, had become a very good personal friend, and remains so to this day. I would often meet him in the Central Lobby at the Palace of Westminster when we would discuss and talk over issues of mutual interest, and of course the United Nations' agreement to designate one whole year during which the world governments and voluntary organisations would focus on the problems and solutions of disabled people.

Organisations around the world would be encouraged to mark this special year by starting innovative projects. Some people would insist on calling the year "The Year for the Disabled" - Oh dear! - It was the Year of Disabled People. The difference between of and for is self evident. We were not going to do things for but rather involve disabled people themselves in deciding what they wanted and doing something about it. Here in Great Britain all sorts of events were used to mark this special year, e.g. new initiatives, new organisations, new buildings, new opportunities and new employment avenues were opened up.

As Public Relations Manager at Remploy Ltd. - a post I secured in 1973 - the Year proved to be extremely busy for me as 1 was inundated with speaking invitations, and my diary rapidly filled up, so much so that I had to turn down an invitation to undertake a public-speaking tour of Australia sponsored by the Australian Government. Her Majesty the Queen also marked the "Year" by holding a Garden Party at Buckingham Palace, to which my wife and I were invited. Despite torrential rain on the day of the Garden Party it was a wonderful day for us both and we were honoured to be guests for tea in the Royal Pavilion along with the members of the Royal Family, We were thrilled to spend some time talking with the Princess of Wales, Lord Snowdon and others; it was the year that Prince Charles and Lady Diana were married.

Of the many things I was engaged in that year, one which gave me much satisfaction was the launching of a major Poster campaign. Having designed and worded the poster, it was pleasing to see it appearing all over the country; in fact, it was referred to in the House of Commons by the then Minister for the Disabled, Mr. Hugh Rossi MP. You can see from the words on the poster and the people in the picture that its message is about integration and that disability is no respecter of people. You can see from the picture that we succeeded in enlisting the co-operation and support of both well-known and unknown individuals to tell the message - Gordon Banks (ex England Goalkeeper), Duncan Goodhew (ex Olympic swimming Gold Medallist), the late Corbett Woodall (BBC. Television Newsreader) and some ordinary people like myself.

As I travelled around the country I had to keep reminding myself and others that, although the special year would come to an end on 31st December 1981, all the problems associated with disability would unfortunately linger on - the year would be over but the malady would continue.

People would often ask me whether I thought the Year had done any good. I often replied that they would have to ask me the same question in ten years or so. Twenty years and more have now gone by and one would have to acknowledge that many of the initiatives taken in 1981 have produced the progress intended. One of the most important strides forward has been the recognition of the importance of listening to the views and aspirations of disabled people and to work with them, and nationally it seems that this has largely now happened. It is also perceivable that the one-time patronising attitude towards those that are different is slowly disappearing. I would suspect that there would be many disabled youngsters who would not recognise nor identify with the real progress that has been made over the last twenty or so years, but of course, fortunately they have not had to live through these years of hard-fought change.

With the benefit of time and perspective it would seem to me that providing for increased personal mobility for disabled people has not released them from other restrictions of immobility, but other problems were brought into sharp focus. Parking for disabled drivers became a pressing concern - after all, you can't drive around all day without stopping from time to time to get out of the car. Special designated parking areas, suitably located, seemed to be the answer provided you could identify the areas and also identify the vehicles for whom the provision was made. I was happy therefore to have played some part in the introduction of the Orange Badge Scheme. The colour of the Badge has now changed to Blue and the special parking spaces are clearly marked. Oh yes, I know that the Scheme is abused from time to time by opportunistic parkers and that enforcement is very difficult to achieve and monitor. However, the Badge does provide identification and recognition of "bona fide" genuine people in need of these special facilities. It is, however, amazing to see what tricks some people will get up to when they are desperate to find a parking space, and 1 am sure it can be very tempting to use an empty "special" bay when there are no others available. I can remember sitting in my car in one of these allocated spaces when someone pulled into the "disabled bay" alongside me; I sat in my car and silently watched. There was no Orange Badge on the car and the driver appeared perfectly fit as he got out. He must have realised I was obviously watching and he suddenly acquired a severe limp! When he thought I was out of his vision he was miraculously cured of the limp as he strode purposefully away! He didn't realise I was able to see him walk away, as my car is festooned with various mirrors covering all angles of rear view vision. 1 was amused at this piece of play-acting - Ah well, such is human nature, but I just hoped it did not prevent another genuine needy driver from using the special space.

On the National front we had a large group of well-intentioned supporters of our efforts to change Government policy so far as mobility was concerned. Two names stand out from those campaigning days - there was the charismatic Graham Hill, the late world-famous racing driver, and his predecessor - Stirling Moss. These two gentlemen, by allying themselves to the cause for more appropriate vehicles for disabled people, greatly facilitated our efforts to publicise "the cause". On several occasions Graham met me in the Central Lobby at Westminster when we would be making our case out to various influential Members of Parliament. On one occasion we were arranging to do a live television item for the "Nationwide" programme, and I rang Graham's office to find out whether he would be available to help with this item. After sorting out his other arrangements he flew back from Paris, shared with me on the news item, which was filmed at Southend Airport, then flew back from Southend to Paris. Such was the generosity of this lovely, caring racing driver.

When the DDA. decided to move its office from the small premises in the East End to a rather more plush and prestigious location at Blue Star House in Archway (North London) it was my friend Stirling Moss who kindly agreed to perform the official opening ceremony,

The eventual introduction of the Mobility Allowance as a meaningful alternative to the old "buggy" or invalid tricycle was the culmination of all the hard work that many people had been involved for many years, and was a cause of considerable satisfaction to me.

By this time in my - dare I describe it as a career - I had acquired a. taste and liking for the public arena, and was being called -upon for all kinds of interviews for radio and television, both locally and nationally. Whilst this work very much filled my week, I was often invited to speak at various Churches and Chapels around Essex. During 1981, the International Year of Disabled People, I received an invitation to be one of the speakers at a week-long Conference organised jointly by the Church of England and the Baptist, Union. I welcomed the opportunity but was a little puzzled to know why I had been invited. Apparently, something of my reputation had gone before me - oh dear! There were Bishops from various parts of the country and Baptist Ministers from widely scattered Churches, and of course. a good number of lay men and women. I had been invited to share my personal experience. and talk about The Year. The theme of the Conference was "Health and Healing" and I felt, with my disability, I was not a very good demonstration of the theme! I had difficulty getting on to the platform; it was too high and they had no ramps to make it easier; the microphone was too high above my head. After some embarrassing shuffling I clambered up onto the platform, the microphone was hastily lowered to my height and I was able to make a start. No, I was not a good advertisement for the Health and Healing theme but was able to share with the Conference my personal experience as a Christian. There had been no magic wand waved over my head but I had had a revelation of myself as God sees me - this had transformed my life and given me the ability to rise above whatever difficulties I may have. We have to make the best of what we have and not complain about what we have not! I was well received and my words were felt to be honest and helpful.

Charles, who was the Public Relations Manager of Remploy Limited, together with Trevor Owen the Managing Director of the company as we were about to enter "No 10" Downing Street. We were guests of the then Prime Minister, The Rt. Hon. Margaret Thatcher MP. It was an occasion organised by "No 10" to mark 1981 being the International Year of Disabled People.

As we entered, Mr Owen had an urgent call of nature - so I went on ahead and went up in the lift, when the guests were greeted by Mrs Thatcher. She asked who I was and who I worked for. I was soon followed by Mr Trevor Owen where he was greeted with the words "I've already met your boss". It might have done my ego some good, but 1 fear it did my promotion prospects, not much good at all. After all I was only a PR man.

Maria Bartha

(L to R) Lord Snowdon, BBC News Presenter, a disabled lady , myself and Lord Jack Ashley. We were recording a News item for the BBC marking the Launch of the International Year of Disabled People in 1981 in the Guildhall, London

Maria Bartha

Oblivious of the crowds that surrounded us. Lord Snowdon and I intensely discuss
issues to do with the International Year of Disabled People 1981 in London's Guildhall

Conveying the message that "disability is no respecter of people", this picture was used during the 1981 International Year of Disabled People in a major poster campaign and appeared on over 1500 main billboards throughout the country. Lest the significant message escapes you it will be noted that the picture shows both the "famous" and the "ordinary" - So we have BBC Television newsreader Corbet Woodall (now deceased); Duncan Goodhew; Gordon Banks (ex England Goal Keeper) and my friends and I, from all walks of life and with all kinds of disability - but they all have worth.

Aled Jones - the world famous Boy Soprano - tries his hand at interviewing for television during the International Year of Disabled People in 1981.

RESTRICTED GROWTH ASSOCIATION

Some time later I was taken aback when I received a letter from the National Council of Social Service, with what was to me a rather strange request. "Did I know" from my case work with disabled people, "of any instances of people of unusually short stature?" as they rather coyly put it. If I had come across such cases did I think it justified to contact them and ascertain whether there was a need to consider setting up a self-help group for this rare group of individuals? I invited the NCSS officer to pay me a visit at my office in North London so that we could talk through the notion. I must confess that at that time my first reaction was to say a very big NO. The idea of an organisation focusing on "short stature" made me cringe somewhat. I suppose my reaction was more of a reflection of my personal and rather fierce determination to be as independent as possible, and my assessment of my own position was that I didn't need such group support. I felt I was quite capable of managing my own life "thank you very much". Anyhow, as our discussion progressed I began to wake up to the fact that although I was OK at the time and could cope perfectly well by myself, I started to think more deeply about the issues. Perhaps there were people of short stature who needed help and encouragement, and perhaps there was a case for me to give my energies to explore the need for such an organisation. I thought of myself as relatively fit and modestly secure (financially), but maybe I did have some duty and responsibility to offer encouragement and support to those of short stature who maybe were not as well blessed as I was.

So it was that I found myself in the vanguard of forming a new national charity. I had said a long time ago that changing public attitudes meant front line action- here was such a challenge! I had always felt there were too many disability charities in the country and I was a little hesitant about starting yet another one. However, I found after some research that there were none that even recognised there were people with these kinds of unique problems as a result of very short stature, and I therefore set about investigating the real situation. With the excellent assistance of the National Council of Social Service we managed to identify about 200 adults and children of restricted growth - subsequently referred to as RG's. This we managed to achieve against a background of not inconsiderable resistance to the whole idea of the proposed organisation. Some potential members were very concerned that the organisation might turn into a "Freak Show" Agency or a theatrical agency. I fully understood the fears and misgivings that they had - indeed, I was not without such feelings myself, but having put my hand to this particular plough there was no turning back. If there was a need then I must try and do something about it.

A public meeting was arranged at a London hotel; it was attended by approximately

100 people of restricted growth who had travelled from all over the country. I remember the excitement when the meeting-room door opened and in toddled more and more RG people. A fairly well-ordered meeting followed. Edgy nerves, fear and apprehension, not knowing exactly what was going to happen, all seemed to ensure that it was not going to be a rowdy meeting. Arising out of the meeting it was decided to elect a steering Committee who would carry out a feasibility study and who were charged with the task of making a realistic proposal for establishing such a self-help organisation. Members of that Committee included myself as the Organisation's first Chairman, Mr. Martin Nelson, Consultant Orthopeadic Surgeon, and the late Mr. LK. Owen, then Chairman of the National Council of Social Service, plus two persons of restricted growth.

The Organisation became a registered Charity in 1970 and the elected Governing Committee, with me as the founder Chairman, set about the task of organising membership, identifying areas of need - both medical and social - and setting in place organisational structures so that we could give intelligent and vocal expression to the problems and aspirations of our members. Providing good role models from within the membership was seen to be of considerable importance.

As the Organisation became established and recognised as a reliable source of specialist information, the membership grew from its (dare I say it) small beginnings and was able to give guidance, encouragement and sometimes inspiration. Like any other group of human beings, members would often express strong views, and this was encouraged from the very early days. We certainly wanted to build a platform and not a prison; we wanted to create an inspirational springboard for members' lives, which hitherto might have been limited.

I received an approach from the Independent Television Company telling me they were considering making a Documentary film about the difficulties encountered by people of small stature. I told them it would be impossible to make such a film accurately without a significant contribution by the Restricted Growth Association. Surprise, surprise! they agreed with me. The film would be directed by Lord Snowdon and would be called "Born to be Small". I must confess to some misgivings about portraying short stature on film. On the other hand, neither was I at all happy to let the film project go ahead without any involvement by people who were having to cope with the problems of that situation themselves.

When I had my first of very many meetings with Lord Snowdon I was quite determined to let him know in no uncertain terms what my main concerns were. I said to him "I am anxious to try and ensure that, since we will never know who will actually see the film, it will be one that will encourage rather then discourage any person of small stature who may see it, and not be a cause for ridicule". He assured me that that was his objective too. Very soon Lord Snowdon and I became good friends and developed a very good working partnership as we worked on the film together. It is very nice to be able to say that we're still good friends.

The film "Born to be Small" was completed and shown all around the world and was widely acclaimed as an important social commentary documentary about the way society treats "the different" and observed the similarities between the aspirations of the disadvantaged and those of the mass of the people.

Towards the end of the year 2000 I was pleased and honoured to be invited to become the National President of the Organisation I had falteringly founded in 1970, supported by many others.

> *It is wonderful to report that the RGA. goes from strength to strength, is growing all the time, and the latest membership figure in 2003 is 750. Charles would be so pleased (Barbara Pocock)*

A small group of early members of the newly formed Restricted Growth Association at the first National Convention of the organisation, held at the Bristol University. Charles Pocock seen in centre front row, who was its founder and first National Chairman. and then became its National President. The RGA was established in 1970

Here is an interesting picture. Professor Tom Shakespeare and myself, taken on the occasion of the 30th Anniversary of the Restricted Growth Association.. What make this picture interesting is that Tom's father - remarkably named Sir William Shakespeare was a very early full member of the RGA. He was a well respected General Practioner in the Stoke Mandeville area. Tom is a highly regarded Geneticist and much in demand as a Lecturer and Commentator on related social issues.

RADIO AND, TELEVISION.

As the years slipped increasingly quickly by, I was becoming a fairly well respected public speaker, both about my work with and for disabled and disadvantaged people and about my Christian faith.

I had planned a business trip to Belfast to discuss issues concerning employment of the disabled at a Conference in Limerick. It became known that I was in Belfast and as I arrived at my hotel I received a telephone call from the Television station in Dublin asking whether I would be prepared to be interviewed live on the Gaye Burn "Late Late Show". They spoke to me at length; I think they were trying to establish whether I could speak intelligently and confidently. You can imagine I soon convinced them that I could. They then sent a taxi to transport me to the studio in Dublin. Appearing on the show with the famous Welsh rugby player, Gareth Edwards, proved to be very interesting and in some ways revealed the attitude of people to the unexpected and unusual.. As I walked on to the set after a brief introduction by Mr. Burn there was a ripple of half-stifled laughter from the audience. As the interview proceeded Mr. Burn asked me: "What kind of reaction do you get from normal people when they meet you for the first time?" I had been asked the question many times before, so I was ready for it! My reply was: "When I meet a normal person I'll let you know". The audience were amused and I said: I don't mind you laughing <u>with me</u>, but I don't like it when people laugh <u>at me</u>".

So many exciting events have occurred during my life, that I fear it would sound rather pompous and boastful to list them all, so I'll pick out little examples so that you may catch a flavour of the things I have in mind. For example, I was invited to be interviewed several times by BBC Radio and Television: On the "Nationwide" News programme Michael Barrett talked to me about a product I had designed (page 17) which gave me a little "elevation"! On different occasions both Brian Redhead and Robert Robinson interviewed me on the BBC "Today" programme.

Together with two colleagues from the Restricted Growth Association, Mary Parkinson on her afternoon TV programme interviewed me regarding the setting up of the Charity. On one occasion, whilst visiting an International Disability Aid Exhibition in London, I was approached by one of the presenters of the BBC Open University programme who asked me to consider doing a live interview "straight to camera" and I was very happy to oblige.

In 1988 I was invited to be the speaker at the Annual Assembly of the Girl Guides Association in London in the presence of the late Princess Margaret. Incidentally, I shared the platform with the Fashion Designer, Jeff Banks, at the time when he was presenting the Clothes Show on television. After the meeting was over, I was honoured to be invited to take tea with the Princess, at which time we talked a great deal about the film "Born to be Small", directed by Lord Snowdon. From my humble beginnings in the little village of Llandybie. I never dreamt I would end up mixing with polititians and Royalty: over the years, I had met with Harold Wilson, MP., James Callaghan MP., Sir Edward Heath, MP., and Margaret Thatcher, MP., - now of course Lady Thatcher.

Whilst 1 was working at Remploy 1 assisted in organising "A World Conference on the Employment of Disabled People". The contingent from Canada was one of about 30 countries represented. My meeting with them at the Surrey University brought about my Canadian invitations. Anyway, as one of the Conference speakers I was asked to address the subject of "Assessing the Needs and Abilities of Disabled People".

Although I know there is nothing special about me and my abilities, I feel very honoured to have been recognised for my efforts on behalf of my fellow disabled friends. For example, I received the Queen's Silver Jubilee Medal for my work with disabled people across the country. In 1985 I was amongst those who were honoured in the New Year's Honours List when I was awarded the MBE in recognition of what I had tried to do to improve the lot of disabled people across the United Kingdom. This was a wonderful occasion for me and my family at Buckingham Palace and afterwards at The Waldorf Hotel.

In 1997 I was surprised that the selection Committee of the Snowdon Award had agreed to name me as the year's recipient of the "Snowdon Award" for improving the understanding of the general public and for setting high example standards for other Disabled people. The presentation ceremony took place in the House of Commons and was attended by Members of both the House of Commons and House of Lords. Lord Snowdon, Lord Ashley

(Jack) and Lord Morris (Alf) have all been tireless campaigners for disabled people over many years. For interest I record the names of some of the previous winners of this prestigious accolade: Sir Jimmy Saville; Esther Rantzen; Simon Weston (the much-admired Falklands war hero) and the great scientist and thinker, Professor Stephen Hawking. How I came to be numbered among such an elite group I really don't know - it certainly wasn't my intelligence!

After I had received the Snowdon Sphere and Certificate I said in my acceptance speech to the assembled gathering that "Disabled people need two things if they are to prove their abilities - opportunities and adequate resources matched to their individual needs, and we should be involved in playing our part in tearing down the barriers and breaking the chains of ignorance and prejudice and set disabled people free".

Allan Titmuss

In full flow at the 1988 Assembly of the Girl Guides Association

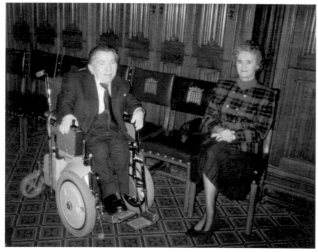

My wife (Barbara) and I wait in the dining room of the House of Commons for the presentation of the Snowdon Award, by Lord Snowdon himself in the presence of members of the House of Lords and Commons.

Barbara looks intently on as Lord Snowdon and I get into deep discussion prior to the presentation ceremony. Lord Snowdon's personal secretary takes a close interest.

Lord Snowdon making a speech before presenting me with the Snowdon Award, flanked by Lord (Jack)Ashley the Disability Rights Campaigner.

Charles proudly holding the Snowdon Sphere, the Certificate Citation for which reads : "For outstanding work for the benefit of disabled people, in encouraging integration and equal opportunities and for focusing public interest upon the needs, rights and abilities of disabled people, with enlightened enthusiasm, sympathetic understanding and caring concern" (Signed : The Earl of Snowdon GCVO) 6th March 1997.

In March 1985, Charles was awarded the MBE by Her majesty the Queen for his services to disabled people.

After the ceremony at Buckingham Palace we returned to the Waldorf Hotel for a Luncheon attended by family and friends

UP AND AWAY

I was very fortunate to make several visits to Canada in my more active days. Many of the trips were organised for me by a Canadian colleague of mine who was the Director of the Saskatchewan Association of Rehabilitation Workshops, based in Regina. I recall flying out of Heathrow on one of these trips - by economy class. When the Jumbo Jet reached its cruising height a steward approached me, grabbed my briefcase and said: "Would you like to follow me?". I said I would and scurried after him down the aisle to what transpired to be the First Class compartment. I was a bit embarrassed having only paid for an economy ticket. As I entered the rather hushed air, when everyone seemed to speak in whispered tones, I was shown to a seat next to a gentleman of portly proportions, and the quality of his clothes seemed to shout "affluence". He kind of looked down on me as I took my seat - I said "Do you mind if I sit next to you?" He looked at me with slightly raised eyebrows and said rather gruffly "Not at all". We struck up a conversation and he seemed rather surprised that such a short, unusual looking person could speak, and that fairly intelligently. He was apparently returning home to Canada after a round-the-world tour, and as we chatted he seemed somewhat nonplussed by my shape, size and conversation. I thought I ought to try and put him more at ease than he obviously was. I said that if I stood up in the plane and offered the other passengers the opportunity to change their physical situation with me, I doubted whether I would have any takers. He agreed. I then said that neither would I be keen to exchange places with any of them. My life was interesting, exciting and very much blessed despite my disabilities.

Just then a stewardess approached and asked if I would like a drink. Thinking that this was going to be very expensive I chose the cheapest drink I could afford - a Coke! My new Canadian friend ordered a whisky. When my, drink arrived that stewardess leaned down to my ear and whispered "The drinks are free in first class". Ah well!

It has been my pleasure and privilege to visit the beautiful country of Canada and 1 responded to the various invitations I received to speak at Seminars and Conferences. I recall on one occasion visiting a Centre in Banff (in the Rockies) and flew from Heathrow to Calgary; the weather was very hot! While we waited for our coach I became more and more hot and sticky but my host said "Hold on, we'll soon cool off when the coach begins its climb up to Banff". The coach, as I recall, was a rather rattly bone shaker of a vehicle with uncomfortable wooden slatted seating. My host was a rather large and heavily built gentleman - I sat next to the window and he seemed to sit <u>on</u> me rather than next to me! "Brewsters Bus", as it was called, set off on this very long and increasingly steep climb up through the Rockies. The scenery was spectacular and picture -postcard like. The bus seemed to complain and I feared it would come to a complete halt, but eventually we arrived at the Banff Conference Centre, much to my relief.

On another occasion when in Toronto I received a telephone call at my Hotel asking if I could spare some time to meet a Doctor. I said I could and he very kindly agreed to meet me at the Airport. Since we had not previously met I suggested that he might find it helpful if I was to wear dark sunglasses and that he could further identify me by the fact that I was only four feet one inch tall! We successfully met, had a meal together and spent several hours talking over shared interests. We chuckled several times over my comments about identification. I was most fortunate to meet very many nice people amongst whom there were a number of disabled Canadians, some of whom were members of the Canadian Paraplegic Association who had strong links with the British Polio Fellowship.

As a direct result of what I had tried to achieve in Canada, the Council and Senate of the University of Saskatchewan decided to confer on me an Honorary Doctor of Laws Degree from the University of Regina. This was in October 1981. The accompanying pictures will give some impression of what was a most thrilling experience. Joined by my wife, I found it difficult to believe that I was receiving such a high award, remembering my very poor educational beginnings. The Award was presented to me by the High Chancellor, Judge Raynell Audreychuk, assisted by the University President, Doctor Lloyd Barber. The venue for the occasion was the magnificent Centre of the Arts in Regina, and the audience of 2000 or more was made up of graduating students, their friends and families, civic and University dignitaries, including the High Commissioner representing the Queen.

Before the event there was one problem that faced the University President - how to get a gown made to the appropriate size given the fact that I was living in Essex and the Gown makers for the University were in Toronto. I sent them a photograph of myself standing next to a four-drawer filing cabinet; from that the makers calculated my size and the proportions of the gown, and ended up with what 1 would only call a "masterpiece" in Red and Gold which fitted perfectly. Just as well really, as I had been asked to give the Convocation address to the assembled audience and it was going out on live television! Mine has indeed been a richly blessed life and I have tried to give a good example of "making the best of what you've got and not complaining of what you haven't got"

The High Chancellor, Judge Raynell Audreychuk, confers an Honorary Doctorate on me, at the 1981 Convocation of the University of Regina. Looking on and applauding are Clint White (Saskachewan Minister of Culture and Youth), Premier Blakeney and the Honourable C. Irwin McIntosh (Lieutenant Governor)

In 1981 Charles gives the Convocation Address at the ceremony at the Centre of the Arts in Regina, Canada, keenly watched, and listened to by the University High Chancellor; Judge Raynell Audreychuk. In addition to the very special "Gown" that had been made for me by the Gownmakers in Toronto, the lectern I used and microphone were positioned most conveniently for my size. I was very comfortable addressing the audience of just over two thousand.

Dr Lloyd Barber, President of Regina University, relaxing after the Investiture Ceremony at the University of Regina, Canada when George Reed and Charles were Honoured. George Reed was (apparently) a well known Baseball Player who had devoted much of his time and talent to aiding young people with mental disorders and he was being recognised for his outstanding work.

The ceremony and reception were held at the beautiful Centre of the Arts.

MY TIME AT REMPLOY LTD.

As I move through this little record of some of the things that have happened to me over the years, I am finding it extremely difficult to keep my story in some kind of chronological order. Different stages and episodes tend to merge with each other and often overlap. Although 1 have referred to Remploy briefly on one or two occasions I think I ought to make mention of the period from 1973 to 1985 which was the time I spent pleasantly and profitably in the employ of Remploy Ltd. After several meetings with that Company's Personnel Director, during which I also had meetings with one or two of the Directors of the Company, I was eventually offered the position of Company Public Relations Officer. There was something of a delay in confirming the appointment in writing because, so I eventually understood, the Managing Director at the time could not bring himself psychologically to accept the fact that I was severely disabled – and obviously so. The rest of the Board of Directors were in agreement that I. should be appointed. Eventually the MD. succumbed to the opinion of his Board colleagues. The first position I held was as Assistant Public Relations Manager, but within six months the PR. man left the Company and I was fortunate enough to take over his duties, much to my surprise.

The Remploy Company had been set up as a result of some major Government initiative with the sole objective of providing meaningful employment for severely injured ex-Service personnel, of which there were very many returning home to this country after fighting in the first and second World Wars.

Remploy had a dual role; one could be called a social responsibility, and the second was to provide an employment service as economically viable. The two objectives, ie. social and commercial, were sometimes in apparent conflict, and this of course was the major challenge to the Company. It had a "Service" and "Manufacturing" capacity within its 90-odd production units. They were scattered throughout the country located in areas described as "areas of social need" as determined by the numbers of unemployed and disabled ex-Service men, and it was my task to assist in identifying Remploy's strengths and promoting them to the public at large.

I drove a Company car all around the country on various missions to do with Remploy. The car was changed every two years, so I drove cars of many descriptions. One at a time, of course! In many was I felt that the bigger the car I was allocated, the better I liked it (the car had to be suitably adapted to meet my physical requirements, of course). Perhaps it was, unknowingly to me at the time, a way of compensating for my lack of inches! I used to enjoy the look of surprise that would spread across people's faces as they watched this small stature person climb into a disproportionately large car and drive off with a cheery wave to the amazed onlookers! I suppose we all have some kind of ego that we feel the need to massage from time to time.

It is interesting to observe that all my major chunks of employment brought me into direct contact with Government Departments and the relevant Ministers - so it was with my work at Remploy. My interest in and concern for disabled people enabled me to promote a number of causes whilst at the same time encouraging more and better employment opportunities for disabled people.

I have hinted earlier that in my view a necessary pre-requisite to obtaining employment is to get a good and sound education. This is obviously true for people generally, but it is particularly relevant for people who are facing life with the huge problems of substantial and permanent handicaps. To prevent or deny disabled youngsters this opportunity (some might even call it a right) is to add a further dimension to the problems facing them. To use an archery metaphor: An individual's quiver should be filled with as many skills and knowledge arrows as possible in order to increase the chances of successfully hitting the employment target. I have always said that academic learning without good social skills training is to seriously damage the young life.

In more recent years I have tried to give my energies to assisting in the work of improving the lot of disabled people in my home area of Essex. Although retired and very much reduced in mobility I still do what I can., For some years I was Chairman of an Arts Organisation covering six Eastern Counties which met in Cambridge, and this was followed by taking over the Chair of an Arts Organisation for disabled and disadvantaged people called Theatre Resource, which seeks to provide an avenue of expression for those individuals who find self-expression difficult and frustrating.

One of the high points in recent years has been my twice-yearly visits to the National Star Centre near Cheltenham for disabled young people, where I had the opportunity and privilege of sharing my Christian faith and at the same time to show that despite difficult physical problems, all is never totally lost. In all these things I know we can be more than conquerors through the One who loves us regardless of who or what we are.

I remember trying to draw the distinction between disability and handicap. I was making the point that in my view and experience people were only handicapped if they were asked to do something for which they were not adequately equipped. You could be disabled, I reasoned, but not necessarily handicapped. To make the point more graphic I said I was going to prove to the students that although their Principal (who was seated alongside me), whilst not evidently disabled, was nevertheless badly handicapped. The students grinned and shuffled about in their wheelchairs; they were looking forward to me making the Principal look a little silly! So, I turned to the Principal and asked him to say something to the students in Russian - I was hoping to make the point that you were only handicapped if you were not properly trained. However, I was made to look rather silly myself, when the Principal proceeded to speak fluent Russian. It made me feel quite small but it enabled me to make my point.

Sustaining me through the many ups and downs of life that we all share, has been my abiding faith and trust in the Lord Jesus Christ for salvation. and I praise Him for all the opportunities He has given me through the years.

Crown Copyright

"Fit for Work" Train Exhibition launch in September 1979. Central to the picture (3rd from either left or right is Mr Donald I. Barnes who was the Director of Manpower and Industrial Relations at Remploy (and my boss) I always looked up to him!

MY WONDERFUL FAMILY

As I look back down the avenues of my life it seems that I have talked mainly about my doings, which I suppose is not surprising really as this is meant to be part of my life-story. However, if I have achieved anything at all it is due in no small measure to the solid, safe and supportive family who have been at my side.

In August 1957, Barbara and I were married at her home Church in the small town of Clydach, near Swansea. Despite the difference in our height, our shared Christian faith seemed to give us a bond far stronger than the doubts some people may have had, although sometimes unexpressed. One day, a Church Pastor met me, and a little while later met Barbara, and he almost exploded with incredulity at how lovely my wife was, and said, unable to contain himself, "Is this your wife?" Was he jealous of me or unbelieving of my charms rather than my appearance? I have long since forgiven him - after all., I have had years to get used to that kind of reaction.

Barbara and I were blessed with two beautiful daughters - Helen Elizabeth and Nicola Ruth. I recall visiting my wife after the birth of our first daughter (Helen). You can probably imagine our apprehension when we knew that Helen was on the way. Although we had been assured that all would be well, we asked ourselves over and over again whether perhaps my condition was genetically inherited. When I called at the Glanamman Maternity Hospital and took this little bundle in my arms I could hardly contain my joy and relief. Helen was beautiful and perfectly formed in every way. This joy was, of course repeated nearly three years later when Nicola was born. I jokingly used to say that the girls had my wife's looks but my brains! Only a joke you understand.

As the girls grew up, they were encouraged not only to go to Sunday School, but also to the Services on Sunday, and learn something of reverence and worship. In their teenage years they belonged to a Young People's

Fellowship at Church and on several occasions joined a Choir in support of the Dick Saunders Evangelistic Missions that were held at various venues in South East Essex.

Helen now lives in Saffron Walden and has three fine sons, though sadly her marriage has recently ended in divorce. Simon (aged 20) is doing well in his employment as Creative Director in a Design Company; Jonathan (aged 18) is studying music at Cardiff College of Music (trumpet and cornet-playing being his speciality); and Peter (aged 17) is studying for "A" levels at the County High School in Saffron Walden. Helen is at present a Beauty Therapist.

Nicola and Mark (our son-in-law) live in a beautiful Grade 2 Listed farmhouse in Thorpe Bay. It has six acres of landscaped grounds, and they enjoy keeping horses, goats, dogs, two aviaries of birds, etc. They have three children: Andrew (aged 18) who is doing a Business Studies Course at Leicester University; Emily (aged 17) who is training to be a Veterinary Nurse, and Joanna (aged 11), who was at Thorpe Hall School now at Southend High School and working very hard! Nicola ran The London Marathon and the Great North Run in 1998, in support of various charities.

Surrounded by such a loving and generous family, and reviewing my life, I can note with a great deal of love, joy and satisfaction the following "footsteps in the sands of time":- When I became a Christian; When I married my lovely wife, Barbara;

The birth of my two lovely daughters, and (strange though this may sound) When I was given an electrically-powered wheelchair by a very good friend. The difference this made to my life in these latter years cannot be fully appreciated, other than being in that position yourself. Strangely, when I used to struggle to walk, people would stare and sometimes jeer, but when I took to the wheelchair people started treating me like a human being, rather than an oddity.

I can truly thank the Lord for the good life I've had, and for the family and many friends who have so patiently smoothed my path. Would I change anything? No, definitely not. Would I want anyone to go through what I have been through? No, definitely not.

Someone said to me on one occasion when I was attending a rather "posh do" in the West End of London, "I do admire you - you come here, we don't know you and you don't know us, and yet you move so easily among us". I replied: "Well, it's like this - I've met myself before, and my disability does not embarrass me at all. If it causes you some difficulty, then I'm afraid you've got the problem and not me"